Dinosaur Plant-eaters

by Leonie Bennett

Editorial consultant: Mitch Cronick

Copyright © **ticktock Entertainment Ltd 2006**
First published in Great Britain in 2006 by **ticktock Media Ltd.,**
Unit 2, Orchard Business Centre, North Farm Road, Tunbridge Wells, Kent TN2 3XF

We would like to thank: Shirley Bickler and Suzanne Baker

ISBN 1 86007 968 7 pbk
Printed in China

Picture credits
t=top, b=bottom, c=centre, l-left, r=right, OFC= outside front cover
Corbis: Page 13. Dinosaur artwork: ticktock Media Ltd.

CONTENTS

Dinosaur plant-eaters

Plant-eating dinosaurs were the
biggest animals that ever
lived on land.

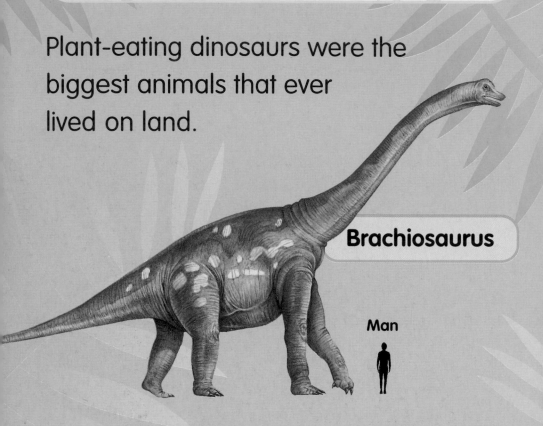

Brachiosaurus

Man

This dinosaur was the biggest
dinosaur we know about.

Seismosaurus

Man

This is the skeleton of a plant-eating dinosaur.

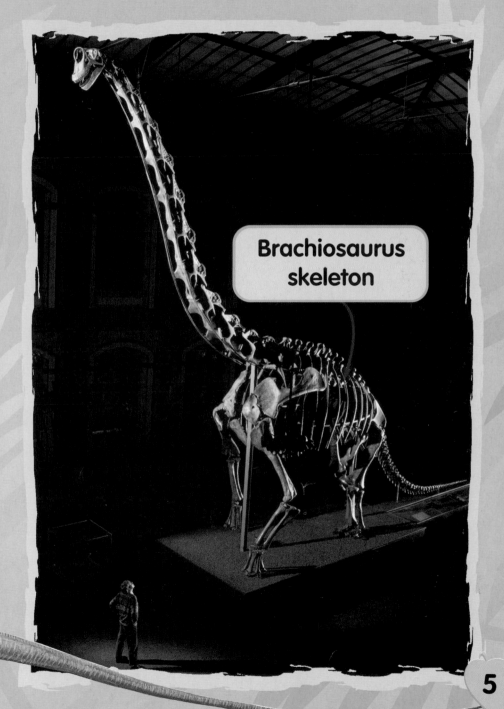

Brachiosaurus skeleton

What did plant-eaters look like?

Plant-eaters walked on four legs.

Some plant-eaters had long necks and small heads.

Armour

Spikes

Some plant-eaters had armour or spikes.

Some meat-eating dinosaurs tried to eat plant-eaters.

The plant-eaters' armour protected them.

Dinosaur food

Plant-eating dinosaurs ate trees, ferns and other plants.

Ferns

Trees

Plants

How did plant-eaters get their food?

Some ate plants on the ground.

Some ate leaves from
the trees.

They used their long
necks to get the leaves.

Diplodocus (dip-low-doh-cus)

This dinosaur needed lots of food.

It had to eat all the time.

It had four, big, strong legs.

Dinosaur size

Man

It had a long tail.

It used its tail to hit other dinosaurs.

Diplodocus

13

Stegosaurus (steg-o-sor-us)

This dinosaur had lots of armour.

It had plates on its back.

It had spikes on its tail.

It used its tail to hit other dinosaurs.

It moved very slowly.

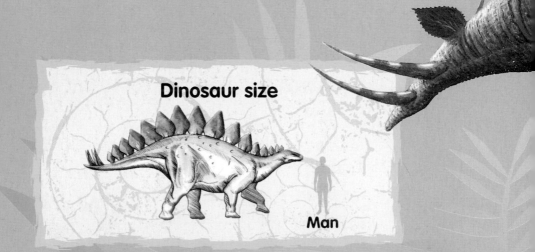

Dinosaur size

Man

Plates

Stegosaurus

15

Triceratops (try-serra-tops)

This dinosaur had a frill made of bone.

The frill stopped other dinosaurs from grabbing its neck.

Triceratops

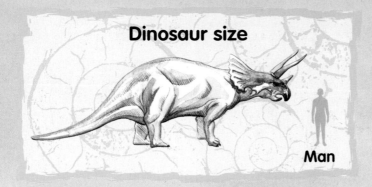

Dinosaur size

Man

It had three horns on its head.

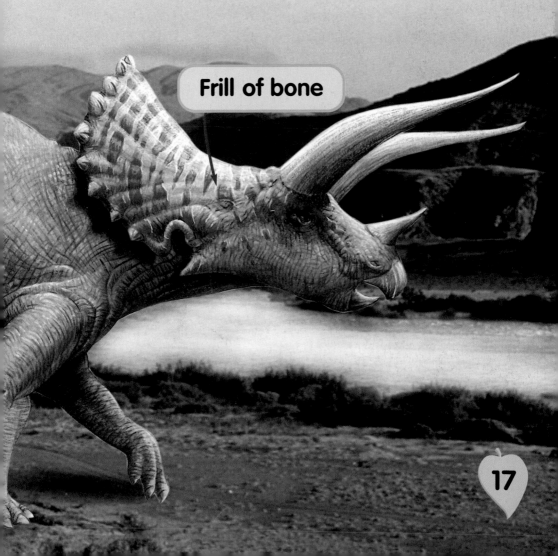

Frill of bone

Euoplocephalus
(you-o-plo-seffa-lus)

This dinosaur had lots of armour.

It had big spikes.

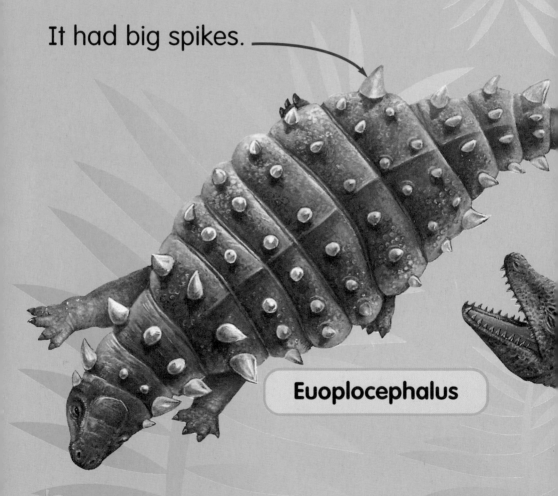

Euoplocephalus

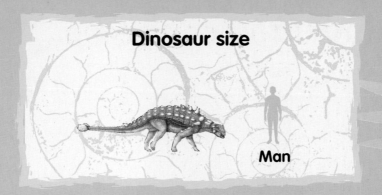

Dinosaur size

Man

It had a club on the end of its tail.

It used its tail to hit other dinosaurs.

Club

19

Hadrosaurus (had-row-sor-us)

This dinosaur walked on two legs or on four legs.

Hadrosaurus

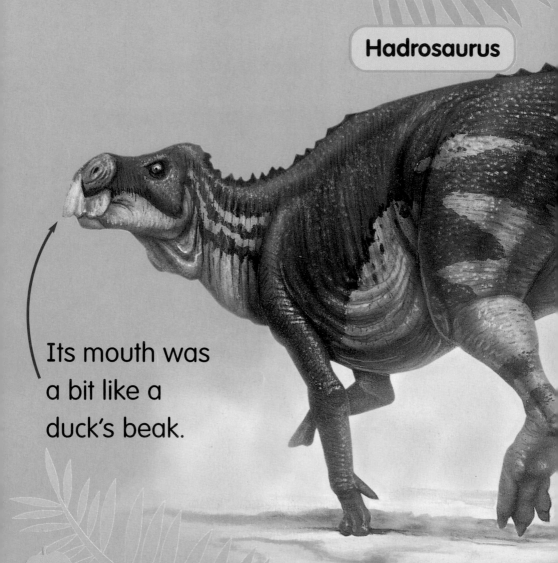

Its mouth was a bit like a duck's beak.

It had a long stiff tail.

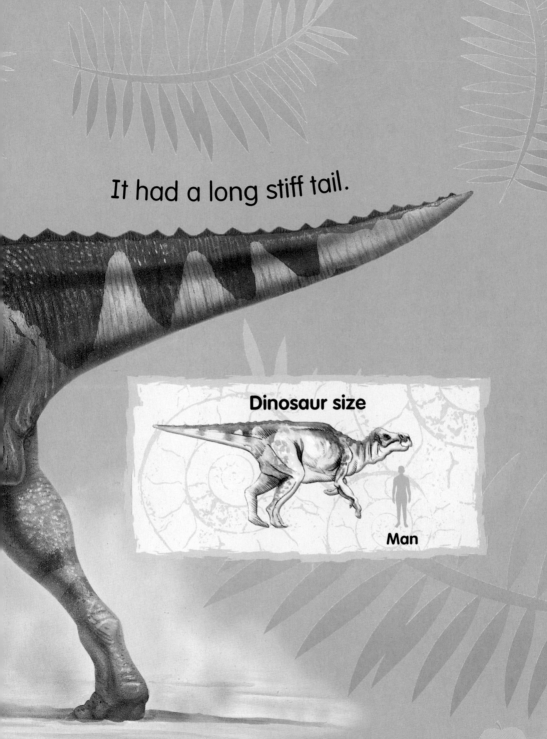

Dinosaur size

Man

Yes or no?
Talking about dinosaurs

Dinosaur plant-eaters ate trees.

Yes or no?

Euoplocephalus had a club on its tail

Yes or no?

Triceratops had plates on its back.

22

Yes or no?

Diplodocus was the biggest dinosaur we know about.

Yes or no?

Which plant-eating dinosaur would you like to meet?

Why?

Activities

What did you think of this book?

 Brilliant    **Good**   **OK**

Which page did you like best? Why?

• • • • • • • • • • • • • •

Which of these dinosaurs is the smallest?
Which is the biggest?

Brachiosaurus • Triceratops • Euoplocephalus

• • • • • • • • • • • • • •

Invent a dinosaur! Draw a big picture
and label it. Use these words:

horn • plates • spikes • tail

• • • • • • • • • • • • • •

Who is the author of this book?
Have you read *Dinosaur Hunters* by
the same author?